Conversations with Philip K. Dick
by Tessa B. Dick

Copyright 2016, 2017 Tessa B. Dick

Portions of this text were previously published on Amazon Kindle under the title "Story Time with Philip K. Dick". Those portions are identified as such and located at the end of this volume.

All photographs in this volume are the work of the author, or used by permission or in the public domain.

Chapter One

Put yourself in the seat next to Philip K. Dick, or across the table from him, and join the conversation. You will learn about how he viewed life and what his work meant to him. You will laugh, cry and shake your head when he goes from happy memories to sad, and then he becomes a clown. Phil loved to play pranks, and sometimes they were not very funny. He also had a habit of winning arguments by denying the evidence.

For example, one time he poured two glasses of wine while I was in the bathroom, and then he asked me to taste them and say which one I preferred. One of the glasses held wine that had spoiled, but I couldn't tell because I had just brushed my teeth with a mint toothpaste. Phil ridiculed me for not being able to tell that the wine was spoiled, instead of realizing and allowing for the fact that I had little experience with wine at age 18. Fortunately, I had taken only a sip from each glass of wine.

Then there was the time when Phil ridiculed a young woman for insisting that they have milk bars in England. She thought that the movie *A Clockwork Orange* was more realistic than science fiction, and Phil insisted that it was not. The movie had the characters going to a milk bar, and Phil insisted that there was no such thing. Well, Phil was wrong. Milk Bar is a restaurant chain that began with a small shop that sold single servings of milk. But he won the argument by using ridicule as a weapon. A loud voice and a condescending attitude often help to win an argument, even when you are wrong.

Phil suffered from chronic boredom, since reality did not satisfy his craving for intellectual stimulation. He couldn't fit in with the academic crowd because he found them limited by specialization. For example, biologists rarely discussed poetry, while musicians rarely discussed astronomy. Although he preferred to spend time with ordinary people, he did admire academics like Dr. Willis McNelly of California State College, Fullerton, who could recite

Chaucer at length. He also liked librarians because, like him, they loved books.

I find myself in a race against time in my efforts to communicate the many ideas put forth by my husband Philip K. Dick. As I grow older, I often find myself reflecting on the fact that the alternative to growing old is unacceptable but inevitable. So before I leave this Earth, I want to give to you the knowledge that was given to me, insofar as I am able to remember it and put it down in words on paper. Do not let this knowledge fade away in the mists of time and forgetfulness. Hold it close and savor it.

Take these words and make them your own. Place yourself on the couch next to Philip K.

Dick and listen to his words. Do not accept the whole cloth of the fabric that he weaves. Listen critically and take away whatever concepts work for you. Weave your own tapestry from his words and your thoughts.

Please keep in mind that, however hard I might try to keep my own ideas separate from Phil's, some will creep in without my conscious knowledge, while others will issue from my own mouth in the pages that follow.

Philip K. Dick educated himself in public libraries after he dropped out of college, and he learned a great deal by discussing his ideas with a variety of people. His close friendship with Bishop James Pike in the early 1960s informed much of his religious thought. Pike, the Episcopal Bishop of California, was forced to resign when the church tried him for heresy. He later died under mysterious circumstances in the Israeli desert, where he had gone to prove that Jesus did not die on the cross.

Phil was intrigued by the Gnostic flavor of Pike's thoughts on religion, but he belonged more securely to the dualist religions. He was also fascinated with the occult. In the 1960s, he and his wife Nancy attended two seances in which Pike tried to contact the spirit of his dead son through a medium. Pike acknowledged them in his book *The Other Side*, which chronicled his attempts to contact Jim Jr., who had committed suicide.

Phil said that a medium did contact something, but it was evil and definitely not human.

Phil's experiences of 1971 and later sent him on a paranoid journey through oppression and flight, abduction and further flight. His paranoia seemed justified, under the circumstances, and his mystical visions provided some comfort. He claimed that his painful childhood pushed him into depression, first because his twin sister died as an infant, and then because his mother Dorothy failed to comfort him when he was sad or hurt. She simply did not know how to empathize. Perhaps it was her own upbringing by a strict English mother that made her seem cold to a needy young boy.

In any case, Phil never quite believed that his mother ever truly loved him. He believed that she blamed him for his sister's death, and he felt guilty about having survived when Jane did not.

Beginning in 1974, he worked on a massive project that he called "Exegesis". This exploration of religion and the paranormal runs to thousands of pages, some handwritten but most typed on a manual typewriter. Phil began his career using a Hermes portable typewriter that his favorite aunt, Dorothy's sister Marion, gave him. He bought his Olympia upright typewriter in 1964 with royalties from his Hugo award-winning novel *The Man in the High Castle*, and he used it till the end of his life. He never had a computer and never wanted one. He never even wanted an electric typewriter. Phil claimed that if it was too easy to type, he would write too much and end up with nonsense.

When I met him in July 1972, he was a broken man. The events of 1971 included surveillance on Phil and his house, numerous burglaries, and confrontations with law enforcement officers who believed that he must be guilty of something, even though they had no evidence. Those troubles culminated in a home invasion that happened while nobody was at home. His house was torn apart, and he was terrorized.

November 17, 1971 became an anniversary

that sent him into panic, followed by depression, every year. He feared that it would happen again. Since he never knew who did it or why, he didn't know how to prevent another attack.

Chapter Two

Imagine a small furnished apartment in the sleepy college town of Fullerton, California. You sit down on an ugly but serviceable blue fabric sofa that shows signs of wear from years of use by multiple tenants. Sinking into the soft foam cushions, you realize that you will have to scoot forward to reach for a glass of wine. Philip K. Dick has poured Mondavi Cabernet Sauvignon, vintage 1970, for everyone.

He found it at Trader Joe's, a little market owned by the Pronto chain, and he considers it a fine California wine. In fact, he says that you pay so much in fees and taxes to import a French wine that you get more for your money with a domestic vintage.

Tim Powers sits on the floor on the opposite side of the coffee table, doodling on a white napkin with a black felt pen. His sketches of knights and dragons lead you to believe that he will find work as an illustrator, but he is actually working on his first novel, *The Drawing of the* Dark. Tim's genre is called "sword and sorcery", a sort of fantasy set most often in the Middle Ages. Several decades later, Disney will buy the movie rights to one of his novels for their *Pirates of the Caribbean* film franchise.

Mary is sitting in the orange easy chair in front of the window. She is tall and thin with bright red hair, and you are pretty sure that she uses hair dye. You can't find the right words to express why you don't like her. Perhaps she reminds you of some girls in high school, the bullies who used to tease you about your clothes, your hair and your lack of a boyfriend. You feel pretty much the same way about Linda, and you simply cannot come up with a reason for those feelings. They are intuitive, not rational.

Later developments confirm your opinion of Mary when she screams hysterically and runs outside because you criticized her acting skills. She is studying acting at Cal State Fullerton, and she wants to be a movie star. Phil says that Mary shoots speed, which is why she always wears long sleeves. She's hiding the "track marks", the needle scars on her arms.

You learn that you are also right about Linda when she is visiting and drinking a cup of coffee. A small green lace-wing lands on the coffee table, and Linda kills it by swatting it with a magazine. You would have picked up the little insect and put it outside.

A couple weeks later, Linda calls in a panic because there's a spider in her bathroom. You, Phil and Tim Powers walk down the street to her nearby apartment to help her. When Phil tells her that it's just a harmless mosquito hawk, Linda says, "If I'd known it was harmless, I would have killed it myself."

Joel pulls up a chair from beside the kitchen table and sets it down next to Tim Powers. Joel lives next door, where Phil used to share his apartment before he met Tessa. Merry Lou sits on the other end of the sofa, and Phil sits between the two of you. Joel likes Phil, but he does not like you. He reminds Phil about the time when they got drunk on tequila sunrises, and the next morning their hangovers were so bad that they couldn't get up off the floor. They blame the women who treated them badly for their need to get drunk.

You like Merry Lou, who seems sweet although not completely innocent or naive. She and Mary used to share this apartment, and they begin to talk about the exorcism that they conducted here. Convinced that this apartment was haunted, they borrowed a book of religious rituals from the college library and read from the exorcism ritual. Phil points out that you perform exorcisms on people, not houses. You cleanse a house or bless it, but you conduct exorcisms on possessed people. He believes that Mary is possessed. You wonder why he lets her come and visit. Phil says, "Keep your friends close, but keep your enemies closer."

The girls explain that they were sitting around the kitchen table, reading aloud from the ritual, when the lamp fell down from the ceiling and landed in the center of the table. The lamp globe shattered, sending shards of glass all over the table, the floor and the girls. This frightened them so much that they gave notice to the landlord and moved out. So now Tessa and Phil know that they are living in a haunted apartment, but they don't really believe in ghosts. Well, maybe they do, or maybe they want to believe.

Tessa and Phil have noticed that one of the bedrooms seems to have a swampy atmosphere. Both bedrooms face the north and have large windows, but while one seems light and airy, the other seems dark and musty. The haunted bedroom is the larger room and has a walk-in closet, so they have been using it. Eventually they will shut the door to the swampy bedroom and use the smaller room. They sleep much better after switching rooms

Tim Powers says to Phil, "Say something Zen."

Phil obligingly clasps his hands and stares at the ceiling. He nurses the pause to the breaking point, and then he says, "The Buddha is a piece of toilet paper."

Everyone laughs.

That saying actually is Zen, and it means that nobody is better than anybody else. As Jesus once said, what you do to the least of men you do to him. St. Paul said that we should show hospitality to everyone because we might entertain angels without knowing.

All of these visitors are students at Cal State Fullerton who first heard of Philip K. Dick when they took a course in science fiction from Dr. Willis McNelly. Phil is not famous and certainly not rich. None of his books has made the best seller list, and no movies or TV shows have been made from them. His one claim to fame is the Hugo Award for his novel *The Man in the High Castle*, but that was almost ten years ago.

The conversation turns to his novel and the madness of Hitler and the Nazis. Toward the end of the war, Phil says, Hitler was commanding battalions and even whole divisions that no longer existed. Did he forget about the many defeats that his military suffered, or were his generals too frightened to tell him? In any case, Hitler moved his imaginary forces around the map of Europe on the table in his war room, expecting victory over the Allies on every front. When the bomb plot of 1944 failed, Hitler became even more crazy. His left arm didn't seem to work properly, and he shook as if he suffered from Parkinson's.

As we know, Germany was defeated, but in Phil's novel they Axis won the war. He spent 20 years researching Hitler and the Nazis before he wrote his novel, and he concluded that the Nazis had seized control of the American government, particularly because they had so many agents in the CIA. In other words, Germany lost but the Nazis won.

Phil's three major sources for his research on the Nazis are *Nazi Culture* by George Mosse, *The Last Days of Hitler* by Hugh Trevor-Roper and *Hitler: A Study in Tyranny* by Alan Bullock. Unfortunately, Trevor-Roper's book is a piece of British propaganda. Despite the book's conclusion that Hitler died in the bunker, Phil suspects that he killed a double and then escaped to South America. However, since Hitler was insane, Martin Bormann and other top Nazis pushed him to the side. They trotted him out occasionally to inspire the movement, but Bormann made the decisions.

Did Hitler have syphilis? He certainly was ill, since his doctor was treating him for some kind of disease. On the other hand, Hitler was a hypochondriac who would have insisted on being treated for some imaginary illness. The doctor's injections might have contained mercury, which was once the only treatment for syphilis, and mercury causes insanity. The Mad Hatter of *Alice in Wonderland* went mad from the fumes of mercury, which hatters used to process felt. The doctor certainly gave him amphetamines, which kept Hitler awake for long hours and contributed to his madness.

When Hitler finally realized that Germany had lost the war, he ordered his military to kill the German people by flooding the bomb shelters with poison gas. He said that they did not deserve to live because they lost the war. The military refused to do it. There were some things that even a Nazi would not do. They were fine with exterminating undesirables in the concentration camps, but they drew the line at wiping out the general population.

Phil explains that he used an oracle to plot his novel. The ancient book *I Ching* has 64 hexagrams, and each hexagram has six lines. Tradition says that it was written by King Wen of the Zhou dynasty, but it probably had multiple authors over a period of several hundred years. The book is used not to tell fortunes, but to give advice. It contains philosophical wisdom of the ancient Chinese. In any case, Phil found it useful for plotting *The Man in the High Castle*.

"It wouldn't give me an ending," he says. "It just spouted gibberish, and that's why my novel doesn't have any real ending. It just sort of stops."

Phil picks up three pennies from the coffee table and tosses them like a pair of dice. Then he draws a line on a small notepad and writes a number next to the line. He repeats this ritual six times, and then he opens the *I Ching*. He has three different translations of this ancient Chinese oracle, but his favorite is the beat-up yellow hardcover edition that he calls "Wilhelm-Baynes". Wilhelm translated the Chinese text into German, and Baynes translated the German text into English. The hexagram that Phil finds in the book is called "Tui over Tui", or "Joy over Joy". You don't remember which line he read. From time to time, Phil says that the oracle is evil, and he will not use it any more. But he will change his mind and cast more hexagrams.

People start telling jokes, and Tessa tries to join in by reciting a routine of Redd Foxx that she has memorized. They don't think it's funny when a white girl tells the same jokes that the black man told. Then she tries some of Joan Rivers' jokes, but they think that she is anti-Semitic because, unlike Joan, she is not Jewish.

Phil tells a "swiftie", a joke based on puns, "Ouch! That hurts, Christ said crossly."

Tessa makes up another swiftie, "My mother was a virgin, Christ said Mary-ly (merrily)."

"Maybe the Nazis hit my house," Phil says. "There are a lot of Neo-Nazis in the Bay Area."

He quickly discards that theory and points out, "My lawyer said it was the government. No doubt about it. They read my books and decided that I was a subversive, a radical, an enemy of the state."

The conversation lasts until well past midnight. Tessa clears the wine glasses from the coffee table, rinses them out and places them in the dish drainer to dry. Tomorrow morning she will drag herself out of bed when she really wants to sleep longer, and she will cook bacon and eggs for breakfast. She also puts on a pot of coffee, but she believes that there is not enough coffee in the world to fully wake her up.

Phil begins to write a story for his friend Ray Nelson, who is putting together a short story anthology. Ray desperately needs that story to satisfy his publisher that the book is worth buying. The problem is that he has committed Phil to following a plot that he does not like; the story has to be about Mary Magdalene mourning the death of Jesus. Phil does not buy into the legend that Jesus was married to Mary Magdalene or any other woman. He writes a paragraph-long scene in which a tear rolls down her cheek, but he is unable to continue writing. Instead he picks up a pen and scrawls a note below the typed text, saying that he has gone mad and is no longer able to write, seals it up in an envelope and mails it to Ray Nelson. Phil's exact words are, "My brains are fried."

Rumors about his mental condition have been spreading through conventions and other gatherings of science fiction fans. They believe that Phil is destroying his mind and his health with street drugs. Actually, Phil has little experience with illegal drugs. He was once addicted to methamphetamine, but it was a prescription from his doctor. At first he tries to dispel the rumors, but finally he gives up and decides that negative publicity is still publicity. He remains angry with Harlan Ellison for claiming that Phil wrote his story "Faith of Our Fathers" under the influence of drugs. That story appeared in Ellison's anthology *Dangerous Visions*, and it describes a government program to control the masses by adding drugs to the water supply.

After a few weeks of losing sleep to late-night conversations, Tessa starts serving dry cereal for breakfast. The thought of cooking bacon and eggs, not to mention eating them, simply makes her feel queasy when she's that tired. Years later, when a British interviewer asks her what Phil's favorite breakfast was, she replies, "Rice Krispies", mostly because she is annoyed at the lack of substantive questions. They failed to ask about Phil's creative process, instead focusing on the mundane details of life in any ordinary household.

A friend who has some experience with the media comments, "That's the BBC for you." In the 1990s, they actually have the nerve to insist that they must interview Tessa in her kitchen. She successfully declines and meets them at the university where she teaches, without embarrassing herself by admitting that she is homeless and sleeping in her car. She has two jobs, but she can't quite come up with the deposits to rent an apartment. Her crushing student loan debt and her son's need for financial assistance are draining all her resources.

Since she divorced Phil, she does not inherit anything from him. Although she is entitled to half of the money from two literary properties, she has not been receiving the money. It is hard to track down book sales and movie options in the years before she has access to the internet.

Her son gets a share of the royalties, but the estate is not bringing in much money.

April 15, 1973

This is to state that Miss Leslie Busby, my fiancee, participated to a great extent in writing the oscuri of Novel, A Scanner Darkly & its to I owe her one half of all income derived from it.

Philip K. Dick.

Chapter Three

When Phil begins working on his next novel, *A Scanner Darkly*, he refuses to go out at all and tells friend snot to visit. He claims that he has the flu, but it lasts for several months. This novel explores the real events of 1971, including all the young people who used to hang around at the house on Santa Benicia in San Rafael, the poor section of Marin County north of the San Francisco Bay.

Phil sleeps only a couple hours at a time, getting up to type whatever ideas have come to him while dreaming or daydreaming. In fact, he spends to much time at the typewriter that Tessa begins putting plates of food on the nearby dresser and quietly leaving, so as not to disturb his work. When Phil does emerge from the spare room to talk to Tessa, he goes over the plot and asks her input. Every day, he hands her pages to proofread and edit. Phil cannot spell properly to save his life, but he also wants to make sure that his words clearly convey their meaning.

Tessa has some talent for writing, even though she majored in mathematics in high school. When they come to the scene where the car breaks down, Tessa suggests that the engine has been covered in dog poop. Actually, that is an hallucination caused by drug abuse, but it also carries a symbolic meaning. The lives of the drug addicts are destroyed, so even though they keep going through the motions of life, their minds and bodies slowly decay. They become the detritus of society.

Soon Tessa is not only rewriting, but actually writing section of *A Scanner Darkly*. At first she enjoys it, but the work eventually becomes a huge burden. This is Phil's story, not her own, and she longs to write her own stories.

A local newspaper reporter named Richard Staley comes to interview Phil in 1973. He thought that he was just going to do a fluff piece about a local celebrity, a minor celebrity. Phil asks him to help by investigating the events of November 1971.

"Why did they throw all my food on the floor?" Phil asks, referring to the hit on his house.

"That's weird," Staley says.

"Maybe they were looking for drugs," Phil speculates. "I heard rumors that something called Mellow Jello was stolen from an Air Force base. It had to be kept in a refrigerator."

"I've never heard of Mellow Jello."

"It was something going around in the Bay Area, mostly the black neighborhoods of

Oakland. Lots of heroin was hitting the streets, and people were dying from overdoses because it was so pure. But this Jello stuff was different. It seemed to be a disease, not a drug.

"There was also a lot of venereal disease. Soldiers were coming back from Vietnam with gonorrhea and syphilis, and their infections didn't clear up with antibiotics. They were incurable. The CIA was trying to kill off hookers and drug addicts, especially if they were black, so they dumped drugs and disease in Oakland."

Another evening gathering sees Tim Powers, Mary and Merry Lou sitting in the living room. Phil is no longer friends with Joel.

Tessa pours coffee and serves it to the people gathered around the living room. Later she will serve dinner, a dish that Mom called "goop". This simple entree is made with crumbled hamburger, tomato sauce and noodles. Sometimes she calls it "swill" after the slop served to prisoners in the dungeon in the popular comic strip "The Wizard of Id".

Phil talks about the Black Panthers who lived in his neighborhood in San Rafael. While he agreed with their goal of racial equality, he felt deathly afraid of them. They were capable of violence in order to achieve their goals, or if somebody acted in a way that they considered disrespectful. Despite his fear, he shook hands with Honor Jackson when he came to the house. Nancy had left Phil for Jackson, and she was carrying Jackson's child. He didn't want any hard feelings to stop him from seeing his baby daughter Isa.

However, once he moved away, Phil did not see Isa for several years. Even when he settled down in Fullerton, he could not convince Nancy to let him see his daughter. A decade after his death, Tessa would learn that Phil had been accused of child abuse. She never saw any sign of that in him, so she put it down to the rantings of a bitter ex-wife. In fact, the only accusation had come from just one person, and that person lacked credibility. Phil loved children and showed great patience with them, but he spent most of his time in conversation with adults. He craved intellectual stimulation.

Here in Fullerton in 1972, Phil becomes convinced that someone is entering the apartment while he and Tessa are out. Nothing seems to be missing, but small things like magazines and books appear to have been moved. He tests his theory by pulling one of Tessa's long hairs out of the hairbrush and taping it between the door and the wall the next time they go out. Sure enough, when they return, the hair has been broken. Someone has been coming inside. Phil eventually confronts Merry Lou, and she admits that she kept her key after she moved out. She likes to sit in her old apartment and read. Phil is furious, not at her, but at the landlord for failing to change the locks. She gives up her key and promises to come over only when Phil and Tessa are at home. Phil feels relieved that it was only Merry Lou and not his enemies.

One morning an FBI agent comes to the door because Phil had called and asked them to investigate the November 17, 1971, invasion of his home. He tells Tessa to stay in the bedroom. After she shuts the bedroom door, Phil opens the front door to let the agent in. Tessa can't hear anything that is said, but she knows what it is about. After about two hours, the agent leaves. Phil says that the agent asked who Tessa was. Phil told them. Her legal name was Leslie Ann

Busby, and he didn't know much more than that.

As the Freedom of Information Act would prove in 1981, both the FBI and the CIA had files on Phil. His mail had been opened, and the license plates of cars that parked at his house in San Rafael were written down.

"We can trust the FBI," Phil says. "They're patriotic Americans. But the CIA is evil."

Chapter Four

One evening you go out with Phil and friends to eat at a Mexican bar and grill called La Paz. Tessa sips on a ginger ale while they down margaritas, and the waitress tells her that she has to leave at ten o'clock if she can't prove that she is over 21 years old. The restaurant closes at ten, but the attached bar stays open until two in the morning.

After a few drinks, Phil begins talking about former wives and girlfriends. Francie picked out an expensive opal and diamond engagement ring. After Phil bought it for her, she dumped him and kept the ring. Jane, on the other hand, showed great generosity by helping Phil out of a serious financial difficulty. She never asked him to pay her back.

Anne wanted Phil to stop writing and work in her jewelry business. He regretted leaving Kleo, who encouraged his writing. He said that he wanted children, and Kleo did not, but Anne did. Phil tried to please Anne by writing literary novels instead of science fiction, but the publishers rejected those efforts. He also wanted to impress his mother by becoming a literary author.

Dorothy had hopes of becoming a successful author, herself, but she never got her fiction published. She did have a successful career writing educational pamphlets for the government. Phil found it ironic that his mother was writing about child care, when she did such a poor job caring for him.

Phil does not understand why Dorothy left his father Joseph Edgar Dick, who liked to be called Edgar. In fact, when Tessa visits Edgar shortly after Phil's death, she learns that Edgar didn't understand it, either. He said that he was supposed to meet Dorothy and his son Philip in Fort Morgan, Colorado, as soon as he finished a job inspecting cattle ranches for the Grange. When he got to Fort Morgan, Dorothy had moved away, taking the baby with her. Edgar remarried, but he and Gertrude never had any children. Phil was his only child.

Phil met Jameson in Canada when he went to the bank where she worked to cash a check. He gave her a copy of one of his books that he was carrying around as a sort of second means of identification, in case they questioned him when he tried to cash his check. As an American in Canada, he felt that they might be reluctant to cash it for him. He found Jameson attractive, but she already had a boyfriend and was not interested in Phil in that way. She will come down to Fullerton and visit because she admires Phil as a person, as well as an author. Jameson tries to introduce Phil to the music of the Eagles, but he refuses to listen to the album she gave him. Years later, Phil will realize that the Eagles are a great band.

Phil met Joel, Tim, Merry Lou, Linda and Mary at one of Dr. McNelly's classes where they were students. He dated Linda for a short time, but they didn't get along. He also met a few people outside that academic circle when he rented a room in a boarding house. He grew attached to Ginger, a smart lady in her late thirties who worked as a barmaid. When Ginger broke it off with him, he felt crushed. He always felt lost when he didn't have a girlfriend; he didn't like being on his own.

Phil drinks too much in an attempt to squelch the pain of all the losses he has experienced. He thinks that it's okay to get drunk because he isn't driving. However, he can't be classified as an alcoholic because he goes without drinking for weeks and even months. He also smokes a cigarette once in a while, but not regularly.

At home the next day, Phil is playing a Jimi Hendrix album when he hears loud knocking at the door. He opens it to find the downstairs neighbor, who is shocked that a man in his forties is playing loud acid rock music. The speakers are sitting on the floor, and the sound of the music bothers the people downstairs.

Phil apologizes, turns down the volume on his stereo and avoids playing it late at night. He really likes to boost the bass end of the audio spectrum, but to the people downstairs it sounds as if someone is dropping concrete blocks onto their ceiling.

The downstairs neighbors become friends, but not close friends. They have just adopted a baby, and they already have a toddler. They explain that they wanted to adopt a baby who would look like them and their daughter, but the agency told them that they would be lucky to get any baby at all. With abortion being legal, there were few few infants up for adoption. They had the choice of adopting an older child, who would likely have emotional problems, or adopting a black baby. They chose the black baby.

You wonder why the landlord lets them have children, since they generally do not allow children or pets. Perhaps children are okay in the downstairs apartment, but not in the upstairs apartment where Phil and Tessa live.

Visitors from out of town usually get treated to dinner out. When he can afford it, Phil likes to eat at Dal Rae, an upscale restaurant with gourmet food. Tessa likes their stuffed artichoke hearts, which have crab meat and lots of melted cheese. She never had such food before, since Mom always made something with hamburger, canned tuna or hot dogs, if she cooked at all.

One time Phil eats stuffed portobello mushrooms there, and he feels ill after going home. He calls the Poison Control Center because he thinks that he ate bad mushrooms, so they tell him to go to the emergency room. Phil is in so much pain that he actually collapses one of his lungs while hugging his chest where it hurts. It turns out that he was passing gall stones, and the mushrooms were not poisonous.

Sometimes he eats at Reuben's Steakhouse, which also has a gourmet menu. When George Clayton Johnson visits with his wife and daughter, Phil and Tessa take them to Reuben's. You expect some sort of calamity because the first thing George does when he enters the apartment is to take off his jeans. He is not wearing underwear. George sits down, tosses the jeans to his teenage daughter and tells her to sew them up because they are ripped. You wonder just how planned this was, since his daughter has a needle and thread in her purse.

George behaves so badly at the restaurant that Phil starts tapping his hand with the large knife that the server gave him to slice a loaf of freshly baked bread, and looking meaningfully at his guest. They never visit again.

Theodore Sturgeon, on the other hand, is a delightful guest. Ted, like Phil, is what you call a starving author. He has very little money in spite of his masterpiece of a novel, *More Than Human*. His twinkling blue eyes and charming smile could melt the heart of a vicious badger. He promises to show Tessa how to blow soap bubbles in the form of a tesseract when they visit, but they never do visit. Phil doesn't like Ted's wife.

Tessa is disappointed that she never got to see the soap bubbles forming a tesseract. Phil is afraid to travel far from home, and the Sturgeons live in Los Angeles, which is about 75 miles away.

> To Tessa, with love;
> the dearest person of
> all. "metal & stone &
> thread did never live.
> But she — my Tessa —
> is our little song."
>
> Philip K. Dick
>
> September 1972

Chapter Five

Tessa learns that her Mom is leaving her Dad, which is not entirely unexpected. Mom takes her aside and asks if she and Phil can take care of her baby sister for a week or two. After Tessa and Phil say yes, Mom announces that she needs between six and eight months. They freak out. They try to make it work for a few days, but they are not at all prepared to take on this responsibility. Eventually, Tessa's older brother Rick intervenes and tells Mom to come get her little girl.

A few weeks later, Tessa invites her father over for dinner. She knows that he is lonely, since Mom left him with little warning. Phil is beside himself with worry because a student from Dr. McNelly's science fiction class is coming to interview him at the same time. Tessa assures Phil that it will work out just fine, and it does. Her father dates and eventually marries Nita June Petrunio, so she becomes Nita Busby. Her college thesis about Phil is widely circulated on the internet under her former name, Nita June Petrunio. She makes a second visit to Phil and Tessa for another interview, and they become friends.

Then Tessa hears that Mom is sending Pinky to the pound. Pinky is her sister's cat, but Tessa has a deep love for animals. She knows that the local animal shelter will kill him. So she and Phil get a friend to drive them to her Dad's house and get Pinky, even though their apartment building does not allow pets. When the manager finds out about the cat, Phil talks her into letting you keep Pinky. He has to pay a deposit to cover any potential pet damage to the apartment, and he really can't afford it, but he also loves animals. By the way, Pinky is short for Pinkerton, the world-famous detective, a good name for a curious cat.

Not long after they get Pinky, Phil and Tessa observe the landlord walking around in a drunken state, shouting that he is going to kill the man who is sleeping with his wife. Phil knows that Bob Armor has beaten his wife and threatened tenants in the past, and he worries that he might be the suspected man in the equation. After all, he often pays the rent late, and now he has a pet that Bob's wife allowed him to keep. She even allows him to live in sin with Tessa, which is still a social problem in 1972. Moreover, Bob has keys to all the apartments because he is the landlord. Another man has already moved out after Bob assaulted him for supposedly sleeping with his wife. Phil announces that he needs a gun for protection.

Tessa borrows a gun from her father, a .22 caliber carbine. Phil asks Joel to check it out for him, and Joel finds a round stuck in the chamber. It takes some work to get it out. Phil and Tessa never fire that rifle because they never need to shoot anyone.

Phil talks about the farm in Marin County where he lived when he was married to Anne. Her first husband, a poet who somehow managed to earn a living, had bought the farm before he died. Phil believes that Richard Rubenstein inherited a fortune, and he is proven right when Rubenstein's daughters get control of their trust funds at age 21. Phil's daughter Laura will inherit a trust fund from her own father years later.

Anne had sheep, and one year Phil and a helpful neighbor slaughtered two lambs. He describes it with great sadness. After that, he decided not to breed the sheep because they couldn't keep the lambs and he didn't want to kill them.

He also had a traumatic experience when a rat got into their young daughters' bedroom. Phil set out a trap, and the rat was caught, but it was still alive. He used a pitchfork to pick up the trap with the rat and carried it out to the pasture, where he planned to set it free. Sadly, the rat had a broken neck and couldn't move. It was going to die, and it was in pain. He stabbed the rat with the pitchfork, and it was still alive, so he took it to the bathtub and drowned it.

Phil says he can never forget the rat's screams or the look in its eyes. He felt haunted by the spirit of that dead rat. It only wanted to find some food, and for that it died a horrible death. He buried it with his

St. Christopher medal as a sort of atonement for having killed it. St. Christopher was the patron saint of travelers until the Vatican decided that he wasn't a real saint.

Anne also had an old horse named Brownie, a gentle gelding. Their daughters learned to ride on Brownie. Anne had great hopes that Laura would become an Olympic athlete competing in gymnastics on horseback, but that never happened. Laura later explains that she did not share her mother's enthusiasm for the sport. In fact, she didn't even want to ride horses. Her mother forced her to do it.

Phil talks about how much he misses his daughters. The last time he went to Anne's house to visit Laura, she ran away from him. He couldn't imagine why his own daughter would be frightened of him. You also have no idea. It's a mystery that only Laura herself can explain.

He wants to see his daughter Isa, but he doesn't know how to contact Nancy, his most recent ex-wife. You learn decades later that Nancy had joined a religious cult and did not have contact with the outside world. Eventually, with the help of a lawyer that he can't afford, Phil manages to have Isa come down to Fullerton to visit him. After that, Laura begins to call collect to talk to her father. But these events are a few years away, and Phil continues to miss his daughters and wonder why their mothers refuse to let him see them. In fact, he is heartbroken and begs Tessa never to keep him away from his child. She promises not to do that, and she keeps her promise.

He hopes to have a son. During his marriage to Anne, she demanded that he get a vasectomy. When he refused, she quit using birth control and got pregnant. Anne went to Oregon, where abortion was legal; it was not legal in California at the time. She got an abortion against Phil's wishes, and she told him that it would have been a boy. He says that he decided to leave her at that precise moment.

Anne later explained that a new baby would have been too much of a financial burden, since they already had two daughters from her previous marriage, as well as Phil's daughter Laura. They also had a big house and a farm to keep going.

Phil claimed that Anne spent too much money on luxuries, and that she selfishly didn't want to give them up for the child. He said that she bought a brand new Jaguar when there was nothing wrong with their car. She saw it, and she wanted it, so she bought it. He also said that she put a deposit on an apartment building that she wanted to buy, without consulting him first. They couldn't afford it, so in the end they didn't buy it, but they lost the deposit money.

Chapter Six

Tessa's belly is growing, so she laughs when the doctor asks, "What makes you think that you're pregnant?" She is four months along, and it shows. "Either I have a huge tumor," she says, "or I'm pregnant."

She wore maternity clothes to her wedding, a simple affair in the living room of their Quartz Lane apartment. They didn't want a lot of people or an expensive ceremony. They had two witnesses: Tessa's father Harry and their neighbor Ila Rae. They all shared a bottle of Mum's champagne and then went out to Reuben's to celebrate. Tessa's father paid for dinner. A couple months later, he will give them $100 as a late wedding gift. They really need the money to pay their bills.

When she tells the doctor that she's having a boy, he presses her about what she will do if the baby turns out to be a girl. Tessa stands her ground, insisting that she is carrying a boy, but the doctor and his nurse keep pressing her. Finally she says, "Then I will love her." But she knows that she is going to give birth to a boy, and she says so.

Phil is convinced that she's going to have twins, but Tessa is certain that she is carrying one child, and that he is a boy. She turns out to be right.

Since the apartment building does not allow children, Phil arranges to move across the street to a building that allows children up to two years of age. The only heavy furniture they own is Phil's old Magnavox television set, so they box up their things and move them. They don't need a moving van to go across the street.

Phil won't let Tessa pick up the boxes and carry them, so all she can do is the packing. He's concerned about anything that might hurt his baby inside her belly. He won't even let her climb up on a chair to reach the high shelves in the kitchen, but she does it anyway when he isn't looking. Nothing bad happens.

The apartment on Cameo Lane sits above the carport, so Phil can play his stereo as loud as he wants, any time that he wants. It has a balcony that soon becomes known as the "catio", a patio for the cat. Pinky loves to go out on the catio and lie in the sun. He also likes to greet visitors, and they have plenty of visitors. They are better able to entertain guests because they are paying less for rent than before. The Cameo Lane apartment is only $145 a month, while the Quartz Lane apartment was $170. In 1972, $25 makes a big difference in the household budget. They are sitting on the couch watching the Watergate hearings on television when Tessa goes into labor. Her son is born in less than three hours.

A group of European university students comes to visit, and you cook dinner for them. Even though Phil once told his mother that Tessa was the worst cook he ever met, she does have one good recipe: Hawaiian-style sweet and sour chicken. Everybody likes it. They sit around the living room with their plates of food while Jean-Pierre Gorin interviews Phil on tape. Peter Fitting is there, having come down from San Francisco to meet Phil; he's a big fan. Phil begins flirting with Agneta Nilson, a Swedish woman with long red hair. He thinks that Tessa can't understand his simple German. It's easy to tell that "eine schöne Mädchen" means "a pretty girl", even though all the German she knows comes from watching old movies on television.

Another French student comes to interview Phil about a month later, and he is angry because Phil gives answers that he doesn't want to hear. He asks about the pre-Socratic philosophy in Phil's novel *UBIK*, but Phil denies knowing anything about pre-Socratic philosophy. The student insists that UBIK employed Empedoclean philosophy, and he calls Phil a liar. He gives up on the interview and walks out.

The female voice that will speak to Phil in his visions despises Sophists, and Phil concurs. He considers Empedocles a Sophist, even though he is not listed among that fifth-century B.C. school of Greek philosophers. Like the Sophists,

Empedocles was involved in politics. The student is seriously discouraged because his entire doctoral thesis depends upon the Empedoclean themes in *UBIK*.

Soon the post-modern school of criticism will make it acceptable for the reader to disagree with the author about the themes in his writing. Phil will actually have university professors telling him what his books are about and arguing with him when he disagrees. They tell him that they know better than he does.

Pinky disappears one day, and when he has been gone for a week, Phil talks the girls next door into letting him take one of their two kittens. The kittens have names from the

mythology of India, and Phil can't
pronounce them, so he calls the kittens Fred
and Fredina. When David James comes to
take photographs for a two-page spread in
the *London Telegraph*, he also takes
photographs of Fred.

After an absence of about two months,
Pinky returns. Tessa finds him in the bushes
in the courtyard, picks him up and brings
him inside. She isn't sure, at first, that this
really is Pinky, so she shows him to Phil to
get confirmation. The cat has faded and
looks almost white, and his long silky fur
has become curly. Phil compares Pinky to a
sheep. He soon learns that Pinky has become
a sort of sacrificial lamb.

Pinky does not get along with Fred, so they call the girls and have them take Fred back. Pinky is never the same, and he soon goes to the veterinarian to see what is wrong. The problem turns out to be cancer, and the veterinarian says that it will be kinder if they never let him wake up from the surgery. The cancer has spread too much, and he can't get it all. Brokenhearted, they tell the doctor to let Pinky pass away peacefully.

About a week later, Phil gets pu from his afternoon nap and announces that he saw Pinky. "A pink rectangle appeared on the wall, a shining pink rectangle in the proportion of the golden mean. Pinky appeared as a cartoon cat like Tony the Tiger, the spokescat for Frosted Flakes. He walked over to me as a lay in bed, and he touched my shoulder with his great paw. I think he was reassuring me that everything is okay."

When Paul Williams comes down to spend two weeks interviewing Phil for a *Rolling Stone* feature article, they can't serve chicken for dinner every night, so they resort to hamburgers and tacos from Naugles. Tessa is learning to cook after Phil bought her a copy of *The Joy of Cooking*. She makes a wonderful dinner featuring trout in aspic, but then she discovers that she doesn't like trout. On the other hand, she does like cod and sea bass. She also learns to make some vegetarian dishes when Phil temporarily gives up meat.

Paul Williams stays at Tessa's father's condominium apartment a few blocks away, since Dad is out of town for the time being. Paul interviews Phil every day, and he gathers enough material to fill a book.

One afternoon you all climb into Paul's car to visit the Special Collections department of the library at Cal State Fullerton, the college where Dr. McNelly teaches. When Dr. McNelly arranged for Phil to come down from Canada to Orange County, he also arranged for the library to preserve his books and papers. Tessa is fascinated by the replica of the Rosetta stone in the library. You are fascinated by the collection of *Unknown Magazine* that Phil donated, as well as the many boxes of manuscripts and correspondence that he has collected over the years. Phil will spend many hours over many months helping the librarian to organize his papers.

Back at the apartment, Phil goes into great detail about the November 17, 1971, "hit" on his house in San Rafael and his theories about who did it and why. That afternoon he received a phone call from Hal Kinchen (almost certainly not his real name), asking him to meet at a local coffee shop. After they hung up, Phil realized that there were two nearby coffee shops in that chain, and he wasn't sure which one Hal meant. He called back, but instead of "hello", Hal said something that sounded like "solarcon six".

Phil hung up the phone without saying anything.

He decided to try both coffee shops, find Hal at one of them and ask him in person about solarcon six. He never made it. Phil's car stalled on the freeway, and he could not get it started. He had to call a tow truck and stand around with his girlfriend Stephanie, waiting. When the mechanic looked at the car, he told Phil that it broke down because someone had tampered with the carburetor. The repair was simple and cheap, but Phil could barely afford it. His writing was not bringing him much income. He had to leave the car overnight, so they took a cab home. The taxi driver refused to take them to his door, instead letting them out on the nearest corner. Phil and Stephanie couldn't persuade the driver to explain why he was afraid to drive down that street, but they soon became afraid, themselves.

When they got to the front door, they found it hanging open with the doorknob lying on the ground. The sliding glass door that led from the front yard into his bedroom was broken, and shards of broken glass lay scattered about. His fireproof filing cabinet had been blown open with explosives, even though he hadn't locked it. All the food in his kitchen had been thrown down onto the floor, and his refrigerator stood open and empty. The strangest part of the scene was that cash and valuables were left lying out in plain sight, while some of his bank records and book manuscripts were missing.

Phil said aloud, to nobody in particular or perhaps to himself, "Thank God, I am not crazy! Somebody really is out to get me!" Of course, you are thinking that insane people can have real enemies.

Phil had felt on edge and about to go over the edge for several weeks. Hal had fed into his growing paranoia, claiming to be part of a secret organization that wanted to recruit Phil to help them pass secret messages to their friends overseas. Hal explained that they would insert coded messages into his novels. When Phil refused to participate, Hal threatened to have him killed and replace him with a look-alike. At times, Phil wondered aloud: "Am I really Philip K. Dick, or am I a double, implanted with false memories and operating under hypnotic control?"

Some of his early stories involved men who have false memories. For example, "The Electric Ant" tells the story of a man who is really a robot, but he doesn't know it. "We Can Remember it for You, Wholesale" tells the story of a man who pays to have a false memory implanted in his brain. He wants to believe that he saved the world, but he really did save the world. The problem is that his memory was wiped because the authorities don't want the public to know about the invasion that he prevented. His novel *Do Androids Dream of Electric Sheep?*, which

was made into the movie *Bladerunner*,
features androids who have false memories
of childhood that they never experienced
because they emerged fully grown from the
laboratory where they were made.

Phil goes over the events at the house on
Santa Benicia in San Rafael over and over,
but nobody can be certain who did it or why.
The authorities might have believed that Phil
was dealing drugs. The Bay Area had a
serious problem with both speed and heroin,
especially among the poor and the youth,
and most especially if they were black.
Many young people did hang out in his
house, but most of them were friends of his
brother-in-law Michael. Phil was not using
drugs, himself, but he would smoke

marijuana if somebody offered it to him.

The military style of the hit on his house suggested another possibility. A new hallucinogenic drug known as "Mellow Jello" was circulating, and the rumor mill said that it had actually been stolen from a government laboratory at a nearby Air Force base. That would explain why all the food had been tossed out of his refrigerator. Mellow Jello had to be kept chilled, so maybe they were looking for it. Apparently it was a highly toxic substance developed for chemical warfare. Perhaps it was actually a contagious disease developed for germ warfare.

Not long after the hit on his house, a sheriff's

deputy told Phil that he should leave Marin County because "We don't want your kind around here." He also said that Phil had enemies and would likely be killed "or worse". He declined to explain what would be worse. Phil decided to put his house up for sale and move away. He was already staying with his friend, the author and editor Avram Davidson. Since Phil had been invited to be Guest of Honor at a science fiction convention in Vancouver, British Columbia, he decided to emigrate to Canada.

Phil also considered that the Black Panthers might have invaded his house looking for drugs, but he discarded that theory because no valuables were taken. Besides, his ex-wife Nancy was living with a Black Panther, and Phil thought that there were no hard feelings between him and Mr. Jackson. In fact, they seemed almost friendly toward him.

It always came back to solarcon six. Either Hal really was a government agent, or he belonged to a radical group that was capable of such an operation. Whoever did it, and for whatever reason, Phil never knew. Some researchers insist that Phil trashed the house himself, and Phil did consider that possibility. However, the use of explosives pointed elsewhere. He had no way to obtain explosives, and he did not know how to use them.

An independent film director whose name you simply can't remember starts visiting every few weeks. He brings friends, and he brings 16 mm films and a projector. You watch all the "juicy" clips from *Deep Throat*, and you find it rather disgusting. You watch some independent films that are quite good. And Phil talks about his life, especially the events of November 1971. He is obsessed by the questions of who had done it and why.

Some of their friends think that Phil has simply gone nuts, while others think that government involvement is quite likely. On the other hand, the hit could have been performed by gang members looking for drugs, but that wouldn't explain why they took bank statements and left cash behind. It remains a mystery, and a frightening one at that.

Questions about who did it and why will haunt Phil for the rest of his life.

Chapter Seven

Put yourself in Tessa's place for a while, and witness the experiences that Philip K. Dick endures. They are no fun at all, and they are terribly frightening. Yet they tend to be exciting adventures, at least at first. Some real things do happen, some unearthly and paranormal things. Then you watch Phil embellish, exaggerate and fabricate. He makes the entire experience much more than it actually was. However, the facts remain.

Some strange things did happen, and you were there to see them. So now you are Tessa, and you are the witness.

You are amazed but ready to believe in the paranormal events that send Phil into a frenzy of typing that forms his monumental work *Exegesis*.

February 14, 1974

Your baby boy still keeps you up at all hours of the night, even though he is seven months old. You can't figure out why he doesn't sleep through the night, and you sometimes think that you would sell your soul for a good night's sleep.

Phil bites into a sandwich and winces. One of his teeth has crumbled. He has to go to the oral surgeon to have the remains of that abscessed molar removed. He will later describe it as a wisdom tooth, but it is not a wisdom tooth. It is a molar that got infected. You call and make the appointment with the oral surgeon. Phil has developed a phobia about talking on the telephone.

February 18, 1974

Phil is frightened of the dentist, so he has general anesthesia while the surgeon removes his tooth. He has the prescriptions for antibiotics and pain pills telephoned to the pharmacy, and they will deliver the medications later that day. You take Phil home and wait for the delivery while Phil lies down in the bedroom. He is still under the influence of the general anesthesia, even though he is awake. He can walk, but he is

unsteady on his feet. He can talk, but the
gauze in his mouth makes speech difficult.

You are on your feet in the kitchen when
you hear the knock on the door, but Phil gets
up out of bed and beats you to the door. The
young woman from the pharmacy hands him
a little white bag containing his prescriptions
while you write out a check to pay for them.
You hear Phil say, "What a pretty necklace!
What is it?"

"It's the Christian fish symbol," the woman
explains.

Now, you know that Phil knows all about
the fish sign. You have a sticker in your
livingroom window that displays the fish

sign in silver lines on a black background. You know, but you say nothing about it, that Phil was just making an excuse to look down her blouse. You hand the check to the pretty young blonde from the pharmacy and say goodbye.

Phil turns around to go down the hall, and a flash of bright sunlight hits him in the eyes. That sunlight, reflected from your fish symbol sticker, leaves an afterimage in his eyes. He sees it as a rectangle in pink phosphene color, floating in front of his face. The rectangle is the afterimage of the rectangular fish sticker.

Phil hurries into the bathroom, where he gets a glass of water and swallows his pills. Then

he lies down again, and he begins to have
the first of many experiences which will
lead to his monumental work, "Exegesis".
The pain pills are Percodan, a powerful
opiate, and he has taken two of them. The
label on the bottle says to take one. The
combination of pain and narcotics certainly
adds to the vision that he experiences, but
that does not explain the content.

He sees a pink rectangle on the white wall of
the bedroom. You regard this as the natural
afterimage of the rectangular fish sticker on
your livingroom window. Phil describes it as
a golden rectangle, not for its color but for
the golden ration of the length of the side to
the length of the base. Ancient Greeks
employed the golden rectangle, based on the

Phi ratio, in art and architecture because they considered it a perfect form. Phi is the ratio of 1.618033 . . . to 1, where the long side of the rectangle is the Phi length, while the short side is a length of 1. You can see the golden rectangle in ancient Greek monuments such as the Parthenon.

Over the next ten days, Phil grows increasingly agitated. You both note unusual activity, including cars that sit in the alley behind your apartment with their engines running. You later learn that the police have been staging for a major drug bust a couple blocks away.

He hears the bedside radio telling him to die. You turn off the radio, but you still hear it.

You unplug the radio, but you still hear it. You take it out to the living room and shut the bedroom door behind you when you go back to try to get some sleep. You can't hear the radio any more, but you suspect that it is still playing. Phil heard it telling him to die, but you just heard soft popular music. Two popular songs that you heard were "You're So Vain" (Carly Simon) and "You're No Good" (Linda Ronstadt).

The next day, you ask the girls next door if they were playing music last night. They say no. They are college students, and their term is over, so they soon move out and go home to their parents. The radio resumes its paranormal activities, and they escalate after you notice a yellow van out on the street.

Two men in overalls take large cardboard boxes out of the van and take them into the vacant apartment next door. You had a photograph of the license plate of that van, but that photo mysteriously disappeared, even though you still have prints from the same roll of film.

You later learn that the big cardboard boxes contained electronic equipment which the men installed in the vacant apartment next door. After that day, the radio is no longer the problem. You hear music and voices in your head. You begin to have strange dreams, mostly nightmares. Phil has nightmares, too.

One night he suddenly wakes you up

because he is hissing. You jump out of bed,
stand at the far end of the room and
repeatedly call his name. When he finally
wakes up, he thanks you. He dreamed that
he was a large cat confined in a cage, and
flying lizards were circling overhead. The
lizards were swooping down to kill him, so
he was hissing at them.

March 2, 1974

"Go down and get the mail," Phil says,
handing you the key to your slot in the mail
boxes downstairs in the courtyard. His
agoraphobia prevents him from going
outside at all. He spends most of his time
furiously typing notes about his experiences.
He has become so agitated that he can't

sleep through the night. He still hears voices in his head, even though the radio is unplugged and stowed in the hall closet. This radio does not use batteries, so it is not operating under its own power. Years later, you learn that a strong microwave signal can power up small electrical appliances. You already know about the phenomenon in which dental work such as braces and fillings can pick up radio signals, so you begin to wonder what happened at the oral surgery.

You bring up the mail and hand it to Phil. He flips through the letters and hands one to you. It will become known as the "Xerox letter". You open the small envelope and pull out a Xerox copy of a book review. You don't quite remember which newspaper printed the article, but you think that it might have been *World Net Daily*. There is no return address on the envelope, but it was postmarked in Austria. Phil thinks that the sender might be Franz Rottensteiner, an Austrian publisher and critic. In any case, it is a strange thing to send to anyone without a return address and without any explanatory note.

Scanning the book review, you see that it is about the decadence of America. About half a dozen words are underlined, and those words all have something to do with death and decay. One of the words was "deterioration". You don't remember the title of the book, but either the book or the review had the word "carousel" in the title.

"Put it back in the envelope," Phil says. "Don't let me see it."

You comply, and Phil takes the letter from you. He claims that he will not look at it, but you later learn that he did read it before sending it off with a letter to the FBI. He thinks that this Xerox letter is some kind of coded message that is meant to set off a series of actions by Phil. He believes that he was brainwashed in Canada when two men in black suits abducted him and drove him around the streets of Vancouver in the back of a limousine. After all, that would fit with the things that Hal Kinchen had told him.

Either they brainwashed Philip K. Dick into doing their bidding, or they had replaced him with a double, as Hal had predicted. The odds are in favor of the real Philip K. Dick having been abducted, about 99.99 to 0.01.

Phil considers March 2, 1974, the real beginning of his visionary experiences.

However, he has encountered the paranormal since early childhood. He has even met himself in a couple strange encounters. When he was a child, he got separated from his group on a field trip in the woods. He was lost and frightened, and then a man took him by the hand and led him back. When Phil turned around to thank the man, he had vanished. Nobody knew who he was, but Phil later concluded that it was his older self.

One night he awoke because his then wife Nancy was screaming. He sat up and saw a man standing at the foot of the bed, The man looked familiar, and Nancy insisted that it was Phil, even though he was in bed next to her. The figure slowly faded away, as if it were a ghost or a dream.

When he writes the date as "3/2/74", people in England and Europe assume that it is the third of February, since they notate the dates backwards. They claim that Americans write them backwards. Eventually, most people settle on calling it "February and March of 1974". In any case, that Xerox letter formed a pivotal point in the Exegesis. Phil eventually obtained his FBI file under the Freedom of Information Act, and all it contained was records of his correspondence with them. It appears that the FBI never investigated him for any reason. On the other hand, much of the information in those pages had been blacked out.

Moreover, the FBI did interview him in the 1950s. Phil and his wife Kleo had joined a Communist student club. The agents asked Phil to report to them, simply listing people who attended the club meetings. They said not to worry about getting people in trouble because most of the members were probably working for the FBI. Phil refused to spy for them, and he quit going to meetings of the club. Besides the FBI, a dozen other government agencies also spy on people. Hal Kinchen might have belonged to one of those agencies, or he might have been a lunatic. In any case, somebody did smash up Phil's house in San Rafael and steal the only manuscript of his novel in progress, *Beyond Vision*, which would have been published after *Flow My Tears, the Policeman Said* and before *A Scanner Darkly*. Fortunately, although they took a manuscript of *Flow My Tears*, Phil had left a copy with his attorney. He has already sent *Flow My Tears* to his editor at Double day, and Roger Zelazny has sent *Deus Irae*, the novel on which they collaborated. Now his editor is pressuring him for the finished manuscript of *Scanner*, but Phil delays because he is reading about the split-brain research studies that are just finding their way into newspapers and magazines for the general public. The split brain will form the scientific explanation for his main character's inability to identify himself in a video.

"You have to put your slippers on to walk toward the dawn," Phil announces. "Sophia said that to me. I think she's talking about Empedocles, who put on his golden slippers and walked into the cone of a volcano. He was never seen again.

"Empedocles was a physician who cured people by exploring their dreams. Te spirit is healing me through my dreams."

During an afternoon nap, Phil has a complex and fascinating vision. He sees images flashing before his eyes, thousands of brightly colored paintings that he recognizes as the work of Paul Klee and Wassili Kandinsky. He feels as if he is visiting a museum in the Soviet Union, and he wonders if someone is transmitting those images to him. After all, someone transmitted voices over the radio, and when the radio was silenced, the voices started popping into his head. The visions begin to take on a benevolent tone. He hears the voice of God telling him that everything will be okay, he is a good person and he deserves to live. It is a woman's voice, and she can't tell him who she is because she doesn't know. He asks her where she is, and she responds, "Let me look around. I see an envelope on the desk. It says, 'F. Walloon, the Portuguese states of America.' Two, seven, thirty-three." She goes on reading an apparently random list of numbers. Of course, no such place as the Portuguese States of America exists, but the people of Brazil still speak Portuguese because of their colonial history. Phil believes that this voice a form of artificial intelligence, like the Eliza program that he read about in *Psychology Today*. Eliza read typed messages from humans and sent typed responses that sometimes fooled them into believing that she was a real person, not a computer program. She was named after Eliza Doolittle in *My Fair Lady*. He begins to call her "the A.I. Voice". Phil develops a theory that the A.I. voice is a computer on board a satellite in Earth orbit, and he will write about the satellite in several of his future novels.

In one of his visions, Phil sees his grandmother putting a small blue-and-white cardboard box into the kitchen cupboard. A soft voice says, "It was the bromide." The female voice starts talking to him when he lies in bed. He isn't quite asleep, but just falling asleep or just waking up. The voices that told him to die rattled his nerves, but this female voice reassures him that he is a good person who deserves to live. She reminds him that he is physically ill and needs to heal. Whenever he asks her name, she refuses to tell him. He says it was actually a dream, not a vision, in which his grandmother reached into the kitchen cupboard and brought out a small blue-and-white box. The female voice of his visions said, "It was the bromide." Phil later said it was bichloride of mercury, but when he first told me about the dream, he specifically said "bromide". I recognized the blue-and-white box as Bromo Seltzer, a medicine that is much like Alka Seltzer. His grandmother probably gave it to him when he was a child. In any case, Phil began to cleanse his body of impurities. The internet did not exist outside of government agencies and large research institutions, but Phil had read about this natural health craze in newspapers and magazines. When Becky came to the door selling Shaklee products, her timing was perfect. Phil bought vitamin C and several other products. He was strongly influenced by Dr. Salk's theory about the healing properties of vitamin C. He became convinced that he had been exposed to heavy metals during his childhood, and he thought that he could flush them out of his system.

Later she will say that her name is Sophia. Phil decides that she is divine wisdom, the female aspect of God, the Holy Spirit. Phil begins looking forward to dreams and waking visions. He has silent conversations with philosophers and theologians whose books he has read. He enjoys the visions, perhaps a little too much, but they do provide some relief from the fear that he still

has enemies. Another time she says that she
is Sybil, specifically the Cumean Sybil.
Then she says, "Think of me as Diana."
Patron saint of slaves?
Owl
Empire Republic War of the Spanish
Lowlands, Dutch cities leave the Holy
Roman Empire

(careful)

John Allegro —

[illegible Arabic/shorthand script]
[illegible] K5 —

Essene scrolls —

Synoptic gospels
in cipher —

[illegible] Sumerian
[illegible] cypher —

<u>Book</u> on <u>Dead Sea</u>
<u>Scrolls</u> —
Christian — why
= Persian heresy
Jerusalem =

[shorthand]
other doctrines =
[shorthand]
Neo-platonism = [shorthand]
[shorthand]
[shorthand]
[shorthand]
[shorthand]
(" = persia & egyptian
[shorthand]
[shorthand]
inaccessable
pythagorian
[shorthand]

Sanatoria: [illegible handwriting]

Palo= [illegible]

Baptism= [illegible]
hygenic [illegible] =!!!

Chapter 8

Phil knows that his shoulder will dislocate very easily. It was crushed in a car accident in the early 1960s, and it has dislocated before. In fact, he says that Linda was taunting him about how he threw a tennis ball like a girl, so he picked it up and threw it as hard as he could, and his shoulder came out of the socket. So he must have known what would happen when he picked up a small seashell and threw it at the wall across the room.

One afternoon he starts a heated argument over nothing, and you don't even remember what it was about. All you know is that he is demanding a ride to the hospital emergency room. You are a very new driver, so the idea scares you, but he won't hear of calling an ambulance. You slowly and carefully drive him to St. Jude's, where your child was born. The doctors inject his arm with valium to relax the muscles, and they put his should back into place. They also recommend a surgeon to repair the shoulder with a new procedure.

This seems to resonate with the vision in which Pinky touched Phil's shoulder with his gentle cartoon cat paw.

Phil gets the surgery, and they keep him in the hospital for six days. He says that they stretched the muscles over his should and stapled it to the bone. In the hospital he has an IV drip of morphine. At home he has Percodan, the same pain pills that he got when he had his oral surgery. While he is recovering at home, he lies in bed most of the time. He says that the pain pills barely take the edge off the pain.

One afternoon, he gets up out of bed and walks out to the living room, calling for you. You put down the dishes that you were washing and go to see what he wants. Phil's eyes are barely open, and he speaks in a monotone.

"Our son is in pain," he says quietly. "Call Dr. M. and tell him that Chrissy has an inguinal hernia."

Phil walks back to the bedroom and lies down again. He seems to be in a trance the whole time. He definitely is not completely awake.

You call the doctor and make an appointment. The baby does have an inguinal hernia, and he is referred to a specialist who confirms it. He also has two hydroceles, a type of cyst that should be removed. However, Christopher is only 14 months old, and he can't have the corrective surgery until he is at least 18 months. In the meantime, you must not let him cry because the hernia could strangulate and kill him. They both lose sleep keeping their baby quiet and happy

In Phil's imagination, and in his novel *VALIS*, this incident turns into an urgent run to the emergency room where surgery is conducted immediately to correct the baby's life-threatening condition. The fact remains that Phil had no way of knowing about the hernia, and yet he knew. Something told him about it. When he was fully awake, he couldn't even get the medical facts right. He said that he had heard our baby babbling while lying in his crib in the other room, and suddenly it sounded like the words of Christ on the cross. That was when he realized that Christopher had a hernia.

Phil is supposed to go to physical therapy to get back the use of his right arm, but he refuses to leave the house. Instead he picks up a rubber ball and squeezes it to build up the strength in his muscles. Eventually, he goes to the typewriter and begins working on a novel about his visions.

When your son is almost two years old, Phil decides to rent a house near where your babysitter lives. You have noticed that house but said nothing because Phil seems to be dead set against doing anything that you want. But when Phil picks up Christopher from the babysitter and sees that house for rent, it becomes something that he wants.

He believes that the visions will stop when he no longer lives upstairs because he perceives them as spirits of the air. He feels sad about that, until he has a vision of a little earthen pot spinning around and laughing. Then he understands that he will have different visions when he lives closer to the ground. The new visions will come from spirits of the earth.

You hope that things will work out well, but you are overwhelmed by the work involved in keeping a three-bedroom house clean and orderly, plus the gardens that need tending. On top of that, you can't even wash the dishes without Phil demanding that you drop everything and listen to him. You get very tired of hearing what God said to him today because it is so highly repetitive. You also long to have a clean house.

After all, the people who come to visit never say, "Gee, Phil's a lousy housekeeper." It all falls on you, and you can't bear the weight.

You sign up for a couple classes at the community college, just to get out of the house a couple times a week. Phil's agoraphobia has gotten so bad that he rarely sees the outside world. He is either lying in bed or sitting in his favorite chair. Even when his daughter Isa finally comes to visit, you have to order him to get out of bed and spend time with her.

RENTAL AGREEMENT
(MONTH-TO-MONTH TENANCY)

THIS AGREEMENT, entered into this 14th day of March, 19 73, by and between

Cecil G & Dorothy A. Knudsen and Philip K & Susan D. Dick, hereinafter called respectively lessor and lessee.

WITNESSETH: That for and in consideration of the payment of the rents and the performance of the covenants contained on the part of lessee, said lessor does hereby demise and let unto the lessee, and lessee hires from lessor for use as a residence those certain premises described as

Unfurnished 3 bedroom house located at

3028 Santa Ysabel Street, Fullerton, California, for a

tenancy from month-to-month commencing on the 15th day of March, 1973, and at a

monthly rental of Two hundred seventy five & no/100 ($275.00) Dollars per month.
On April 15, 1973, lessee will pay
payable monthly in advance on the first day of each and every month, 1/2 month rent in the amount of
$137.50 for the period April 15 to May 1, 1973.
It is further mutually agreed between the parties as follows: Thereafter rent will be due and payable on the first of each month.

(1) Said premises shall be occupied by no more than _____ adults and _____ children.

(2) Lessee shall not keep or permit to be kept in said premises any dog, cat, bird or other household pets more than one dog.

(3) Lessee shall not violate any city ordinance or state law in or about said premises.

(4) That all alterations, additions, or improvements made or used to said premises shall, unless otherwise provided by written agreement between the parties hereto, be the property of Lessor and shall remain upon and be surrendered with the premises.

(5) Lessee shall not sub-let the demised premises, or any part thereof, or assign this agreement without the lessor's written consent.

(6) Any failure by lessee to pay rent or other charges promptly when due, or to comply with any other terms or conditions hereof, shall at the option of the lessor forthwith terminate this tenancy.

(7) Lessee shall keep and maintain the premises in a clean and sanitary condition at all times, and upon the termination of the tenancy shall surrender the premises to the lessor in as good condition as when received, ordinary wear and damage by the elements excepted.

(8) Except as to any exception which makes the premises untenantable, lessee hereby forever waives all rights to make repairs at the expense of lessor as provided in Section 1942 of the Civil Code of the State of California, and all rights provided in Section 1941 of said Civil Code.

(9) The lessee agrees to properly cultivate, care for, and adequately water the lawn, shrubbery, trees and grounds.

(10) The lessee shall pay for all water supplied to the said premises. The lessor shall pay for all gas, heat, light, power, telephone service, and all other services, except as herein provided, supplied to the said premises.

(11) Nothing contained in this agreement shall be construed as waiving any of lessor's rights under the laws of the State of California.

(12) This agreement and the tenancy hereby granted may be terminated at any time by either party hereto by giving to the other party not less than

thirty (30) days prior notice in writing.

(13) If an action be brought for the recovery of rent or other charges due or to become due under this lease or by reason of a breach of any covenant herein contained or for the recovery of the possession of said premises, or on account of the maintenance of anything against the terms of lease, or to enforce for damages to said property, or to abate any act contrary to the provisions hereof, Lessee will pay to Lessor all of the costs of such an action and including, but not by way of limitation, reasonable attorney's fees, whether or not the action proceed to judgment.

(14) Remarks: see over

IN WITNESS WHEREOF the parties hereto have executed this agreement in duplicate the day and year first above written.

Cecil G. Knudsen
Dorothy A. Knudsen Lessor

Philip K. Dick
Susan B. Dick Lessee

Initial costs are first and last month's rent plus $100.00 security deposit, total $680.00. Of this amount, lessee on March 1, 1975 paid $180.00 and the balance of $400.00 on March 14, 1975 receipt of which is hereby acknowledged. The security deposit of $100.00 is to be held by lessor and returned to lessee at the close of tenancy provided the following conditions have been met:

1. Lessee remains at least one year.
2. Lessee leaves premises in as good and clean condition as when taking possession, normal wear excepted.
3. Lessee gives 35 days notice prior to moving.
4. Lessee gives permission to show house during last month by appointment.
5. Lessee returns two (2) keys.

The following personal property has been furnished by the lessor: drapes, curtains and rods all windows, TV antenna, fireplace screen, 2 air conditioners. Regarding the latter, lessor does not warrant or provide repair.

Cecil C. Knudson
Dorothy A. Knudson
Lessor

Philip E. Dick
Tessa B. Dick

Please make checks payable to:

Cecil G. Knudson
731 N. Virginia Rd.
Fullerton, Calif. 92631

Phone: 871-7766

Mar. 14, 1975
Above agreement amended as follows: of the $400.00 due, $300.00 has been paid this date and the balance of $100.00 will be paid on April 1, 1975.

One day Phil types a letter, seals it into an envelope and frantically asks for a postage stamp. You find one in your purse and hand it to him. He dashes out to the mailbox down the street and drops the letter in with a sense of triumph.

"The spirit told me to fire my agent," Phil says. "He's been cheating me out of a lot of money."

Within a week, Phil receives royalty checks totaling about ten thousand dollars. He "unfires" his agent. His contract with the Scott Meredith Literary Agency comes up for renewal once a year, and he told the agency that he would not renew it. Since they sent him all that money, he decides to go ahead and renew the contract.

He starts shopping for a sports car and eventually settles on a used Fiat Spyder. "The Fiat is a piece of junk," he says, "but it's fun to drive." Besides, it was cheap.

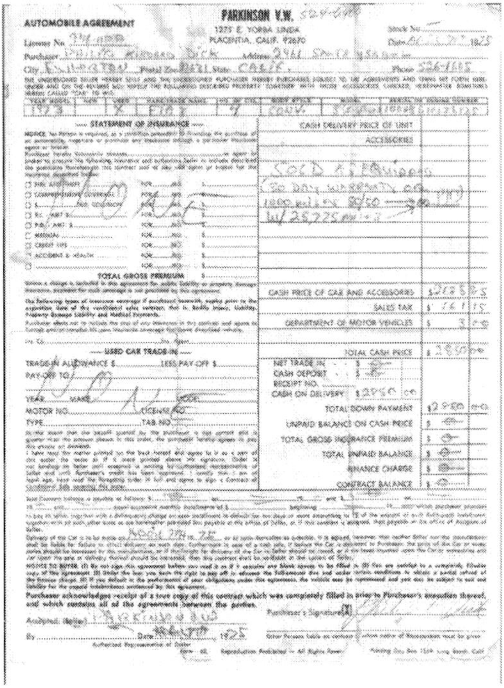
PARKINSON V.W.
AUTOMOBILE AGREEMENT
1275 E. YORBA LINDA
PLACENTIA, CALIF. 92670
Stock No.
Date
License No.
Purchaser
Address
City
Postal Zone
State
Phone
STATEMENT OF INSURANCE
TOTAL GROSS PREMIUM
USED CAR TRADE-IN
TRADE-IN ALLOWANCE $
LESS PAY-OFF $
PAY-OFF TO
YEAR
MAKE
MOTOR NO.
LICENSE NO.
TYPE
TAB NO.
CASH DELIVERY PRICE OF UNIT
ACCESSORIES
CASH PRICE OF CAR AND ACCESSORIES
SALES TAX
DEPARTMENT OF MOTOR VEHICLES
TOTAL CASH PRICE
NET TRADE IN
CASH DEPOSIT
RECEIPT NO.
CASH ON DELIVERY
TOTAL DOWN PAYMENT
UNPAID BALANCE ON CASH PRICE
TOTAL GROSS INSURANCE PREMIUM
TOTAL UNPAID BALANCE
FINANCE CHARGE
CONTRACT BALANCE
Purchaser acknowledges receipt of a true copy of this contract which was completely filled in prior to Purchaser's execution thereof, and which contains all of the agreements between the parties.
Purchaser's Signature
Accepted: (Seller)
By
Date
Authorized Representative of Seller

He eventually leaves you and tells all his friends that you left him. You can't understand why they believe him, since he is living in a newly rented apartment where he had all the furniture and valuables taken by moving van. He even has a new girlfriend. Phil later explains that his enemies were after him, and he believed that you and his young son would come to harm. He was trying to convince his enemies that he didn't care about you, so they would leave you alone. You don't know whether to believe that story, but he does write about it in his novel *Radio Free Albemuth*.

After about six months in which you have stayed with your mother 500 miles away, you manage to rent a room in Fullerton. You start bringing your son to visit his father. Phil begs you to stay and visit with him, so you do.

You go back to school, where you finish a degree in foreign language. Unable to find a job, you continue and get a degree in communications. You went to college because employers said that you were under-qualified for the work, and now they say that you are overqualified. You go back to school and work on a Master's degree in English literature. Eventually you teach English at the university.

Eventually, the university morphs from a place of learning to a political monster. The experience of teaching taught you more than you ever learned as a student, and for that you are grateful. However, serious illness takes you out of work for over a year, and you just can't get back into it. The university will never give you tenure, and the job devolves to where it barely earns enough money to keep the car running to drive to work.

November 24, 1972

Dear Paul and David,

I forgot to ask you one thing regarding CONFESSIONS OF A CRAP ARTIST, and this is so important to me: I'd like to dedicate it, if that's okay, with the following dedication:

> To Tess,
> the dark-haired girl who
> cared about me when it
> mattered most; that is,
> all the time.
> This is to her with love.

Thank you very much, you guys, if you could include this before the text of the novel in the place where dedications go. If I get mad at Tess I'll probably yank it out, but on the other hand no one else probably will ever care about me as such anyhow, so if I do yank it out I'll more than likely put it back later on.

Keep in touch.

With deep affection,

Phil

Philip K. Dick
3028 Quartz Lane #3
Fullerton
Calif 92631

Chapter 9

Exegesis begins in 1974 and consumes Philip K. Dick until the end of his life, and perhaps beyond. He begins to explore the idea of a novel about his mystical experiences, but his agent tells him that he can't sell it. Publishers want adventure, not intellectual theses and certainly not religious treatises.

Phil persists, writing basically the same novel under different titles, producing *VALIS*, *Radio Free Albemuth* and *Divine Invasion*. His first draft is titled *Firebright*, but it becomes *VALIS* when he finishes the novel. The people in charge of his estate replace *Radio Free Albemuth* with *The Transmigration of Timothy Archer*.

If they had asked Tessa, instead of engaging in guesswork, they would not have made that mistake. *The Transmigration of Timothy Archer* refers back to Phil's friendship with Bishop James Pike in the early 1960s. The three *VALIS* novels, on the other hand, refer to Phil's realization that the mythic battle between good and evil is taking place right here, on this planet, right now and forever, among these people.

He envisions the spirit as a littlle blue light that dances around in the air like a butterfly, and he calls it Firebright. But when a voice that he calls "AI" (artificial intelligence) speaks to him about an alternate reality, he concludes that a sort of female savior is a computer on board a satellite in Earth orbit. He calls the female voice "Sophia", and he calls that satellite "VALIS" (Vast Active Living Intelligence System). VALIS gathers intelligence about events in our world, and from time to time it intervenes in our affairs.

He draws upon his own life to fill out his characters. For example, Nick Brady in *Radio Free Albemuth* works in A&R (artists and repertoire) for a record company because Phil was once offered a job in A&R. He turned it down because he found it difficult to deal with people. He preferred to sit at his desk and write. In fact, he suffered from agoraphobia, and often he was unable

too walk out his front door. He fears
something that he can't quite define.

Phil's home was always open to visitors,
since he didn't have to go out to receive
them. He enjoyed stimulating conversation,
even when it devolved into arguments.

He spends hours watching television. He
rarely misses the evening news, and he loves
to watch *In Search Of*, which explores topics
on the edge of reality. He speculates about
werewolves, vampires, the Loch Ness
monster, ghosts and demons, zombies and
more. He also enjoys light entertainment,
including Bob Newhart, Mary Tyler Moore
and Carol Burnett.

Phil watches David Frost's interviews with Richard Nixon. He believes that Nixon is unremittingly evil. He bases his character President Ferris Fremont on Nixon. In the end, however, he prays for Nixon and even for Hitler. He comes to understand that God is in charge, and we don't have the right to judge anyone. No matter how unforgivably evil they might be, their fate is not up to us to decide.

"Pinky saved my life, Phil says. "When he disappeared, he transformed himself from his cat form and came back as a sacrificial lamb. His fur turned woolly and almost white, like a lamb. So he took on all the microwave radiation that was beamed at me, and he suffered the cancer that was aimed at me.

"The CIA wanted me dead because of my left-wing views. They're all a bunch of Nazis. They know that Hitler survived the war, and the Nazis took over American intelligence."

Phil goes back into his speculations about his novel *The Man in the High Castle*. "Hitler had President Kennedy killed for making a deal with Kruschev instead of bombing Cuba. Maybe he also had Bobby Kennedy and Martin Luther King killed. In any case, it was Nazis who did it. Oswald was innocent, and Sirhan Sirhan was innocent. James Earl Ray probably was a Nazi, even if he didn't kill Dr. King. It was

Nazis who killed them all."

Phil suggests that all three purported assassins were victims of mind control. He believes that he, himself, is a victim of mind control.

"They tried to recruit me, and when that failed, they tried to brainwash me. When that failed, they tried to kill me. The only reason I survived was divine intervention."

"Hal Kinchen told me that my television set was watching me and sending videos back to someone. I didn't believe him, but then he opened the back of the television and showed me the camera that was recording everything that went on in my living room.

Phil pauses to take a drag off a clove

cigarette and sip his French roast coffee. "He showed me how to make a silencer out of foam rubber and aluminum foil. I told him it wouldn't work, but he insisted that it would. Hal rolled up this huge tube of aluminum foil-covered foam rubber, and he stuck it on the end of the barrel of a .44 pistol. Then he went out into the back yard and fired the gun. It made a loud booming sound, and his homemade silencer caught fire. I told him it wouldn't work."

Story Time with Philip K. Dick

Imagine yourself sitting on the brown plaid sofa in the living room of Philip K. Dick's condominium apartment. You always thought that you could sit down and have a beer with him, but it turns out that he doesn't drink beer. You sip from a cup of French roast coffee, and maybe you light a cigarette. The air fills with the aroma from two tins of steak and kidney pie that he bought at Trader Joe's, and which are heating in the oven. Phil sits down next to you and tips some Dean Swift snuff onto the back of his hand. He raises his hand to his nose, inhales deeply, then loudly sneezes into his handkerchief. Unable to sit still for long, he gets up to fiddle with his stereo. He plays some Dowland lute songs and explains that he got the title of his novel *Flow My Tears, the Policeman Said* from Dowland's song "Flow My Tears".

You visit Phil in a time of upheaval. The year 1981 sees President Reagan entering his first term in that high office. In March he is shot but survives. In June a severe recession begins, with rising unemployment and rising prices. The AIDS virus is discovered in homosexual men, so it is called the "gay disease" until heterosexuals are found to suffer from it. In August MTV is launched, and they show music videos. Most people still don't have cable television, which is a crude early version of today's technology. In 1982, Israel invades Lebanon. The United States places an oil embargo on Libya for their support of terrorism. The ground-breaking ceremony for the Vietnam Veterans Memorial is held in Washington, D.C. You wonder if the job market will ever pick up, and you wonder how you're going to pay next month's rent on what you earn at the only job you could get.

Phil paces around the room while excitedly telling you that whale songs sound like the music from Brian Eno's 30-foot wire, and he plays a track from each album to prove his point. The sound from Time Windows speakers supplemented with a Bose sub-woofer makes it possible to enjoy the stereophonic effect from almost any spot in the room. However, you don't really enjoy the discordant music of the whales or the wire. You suppress a sigh of relief when he puts on a vinyl LP of Vivaldi's four horn concertos, followed by Bach cantatas and fugues. It wouldn't be polite to complain about his choice in music. Besides, you absolutely love the sounds of Fleetwood Mac's "Rumors" album, as well as Pat Benatar, the Eagles and more. Sure, you could buy your own record albums, but your stereo system can't come near to matching the clarity, fidelity and richness that Phil's equipment provides. He tells you that he plans to buy a reel-to-reel tape recorder and put all his music on tape. Meanwhile, he has bought himself a turntable that reduces the noise from vinyl records by damping any vibrations that might take the stylus off track.

Phil begins to tell you about a story he once wrote. He lost the manuscript years ago, but he remembers the tale of a squirrel who wrote stories on a Hermes portable typewriter. Whenever the squirrel went outside to look for acorns, his wife would scream at him, "The shrike will get you!" This reflects his mother's fear that terrible things would happen to him if he moved out of her home when he was 18 years old. Phil did move out, and he rented a room in a big house where a group of poets and other artists lived. One of those poets, Gerry Ackerman, will visit the memorial that takes place on March 2, 2002, the 20th anniversary of Phil's death.

Phil also talks about his mainstream novels, especially the only one published during his lifetime, *Confessions of a Crap Artist*. The main character Jack Isidore was named after Isidore of Seville, a Spanish bishop and scholar of the 500s and 600s A.D. who wrote an encyclopedia containing all the knowledge in the world in a single volume. It is fitting that Isidore is now considered the patron saint of the internet. But in 1982, while you are talking to Phil, the internet is only a dream for most people. We find information in books, magazines and newspapers.

We spend hours in the public library, and

most of us don't even have computers. In fact, most libraries don't have computers. You search for books in the card catalog, a beautiful wooden cabinet with drawers full of alphabetically arranged index cards. Phil has one of the first cable television services, SelecTV. It has one channel, and it comes in over the telephone line. SelecTV offers movies and sports events that you can't get on broadcast television. Phil, who suffers from agoraphobia, enjoys watching movies without having to go to a theatre. He hates to leave his apartment, and he gets anxious in crowds. He rarely watches sports.

You hear the chime of the oven timer, and Phil disappears into the kitchen for a few minutes. When he emerges with two plates of steaming steak and kidney pie, you realize how hungry you are. You also realize that you need a refill of your coffee. Phil puts on a Steve Miller Band album and explains that he didn't like their music at first, but now he has come to appreciate it. He never did learn to like Neil Diamond or Three Dog Night, but he has a complete collection of the Beatles and a complete collection of Beethoven. Phil was born on December 16, the day that Ludwig Van Beethoven was baptized. You have to agree with him that America's hit song "A Horse With No Name" is annoying. You've learned to appreciate the Rolling Stones, even though Mick Jagger's hype about "the greatest rock and roll band in the world" seems overblown. Phil also likes jazz, and he has some rare recordings of Charlie "Bird" Parker. Soon you're listening to Jefferson Airplane or Jefferson Starship, not sure which, but that is definitely the voice of Grace Slick. When you've finished eating, you follow Phil out to the kitchen and put your empty plate in the sink. He turns down the volume on the stereo and begins talking again.

You visit Phil often, and he always has plenty to tell you about his life, his writing and his favorite music. He frequently talks about sequels to his novels. He never gave up working on the sequel to *The Man in the High Castle*, but he still can't write it because the Nazis were too horrible to imagine. He continues reading about Hitler and the Nazis, and he continues researching the cities and geography of the east coast of the United States, which Germany occupies in that alternate history. He imagines a group of American rebels like the French Underground of World War 2. These rebels plan to win against the Nazis by educating people. They commit acts of sabotage, such as blowing up bridges, and they spray paint graffiti on the walls of Nazi offices, but their primary mission is to distribute a book about the Allies winning World War 2. A German officer tasked with putting down the rebellion searches for Hawthorne Abendsen, the author of that subversive book. The German officer lacks empathy and sees nothing wrong with the Nazi eugenics program. He believes that the old, infirm, mentally challenged, Jews, Eastern Europeans, and any subhumans who consume valuable resources must be eliminated from the human gene pool.

In his search for Abendsen, this German officer encounters seemingly paranormal events. A different universe intrudes upon his world, and he finds himself walking down the streets of New York City where the American flag still flies from banks and post offices. When he tries to step into his office, he finds a discount store occupying the building. People stare at him and remark in whispers about his uniform. After all, it isn't Halloween, so why is he dressed up in that costume?

The German officer will need a name, so perhaps he will be Walther Gerlach, a high-ranking SS officer. As a civil engineer, as well as a dedicated Nazi, Gerlach fits the role of a man who seeks to destroy the high castle where Abendsen lives. Gerlach is also involved in repairing and protecting bridges and other structures in New York that suffer from rebel attacks. When he stumbles into our reality, he is astounded to see the Twin Towers rising skyward; in his time line, they were never built. He also sees the Empire State Building standing undamaged, but he knows that the German Luftwaffe bombed it in the war. And the pagan Statue of Liberty proudly stands on Liberty Island, even though the Nazis scrapped it for war materials a decade ago. The copper-clad iron and steel statue had been turned into copper jackets for ammunition and steel decks for warships.

The United States provides virtually unlimited resources, especially petroleum, coal and steel, which the Heimatland lacks. Labor shortages are filled by hordes of hungry Americans. The Ubermensch finds an abundance of Lebensraum in North America. It is only a matter of time before the American Aryans will come to understand and accept the principles laid out by Joseph Goebbels in his magnificent tracts and pamphlets. The useless eaters must be eliminated because they drag down the progress of the Aryan race. Utopia looms on the horizon like a shining war helmet, and only the hordes of Russia and Asia stand in the way.

And so the story becomes too horrifying to contemplate, and Phil never writes it. He does begin a sequel to his novel *The Penultimate Truth*. That first novel depicts a world in which millions of people live in underground bunkers where they manufacture robots for the war effort. By the end of the novel, we learn that the war ended a decade ago and the robots are actually servants for the wealthy and powerful elite who live on vast landed estates. The people have been deceived by false reports of terrible pollution and radiation on the surface of the planet, so they are afraid to leave their underground shelters. Only the most desperate people dare to venture above ground, where they find a beautiful landscape with lush vegetation and healthy wildlife. Some of the buildings are bombed out, and some farm fields have bomb craters, but the natural world is recovering. Moreover, the harmful radiation that they have been warned about does not exist. It is simply a fear tactic to keep people down in their bomb shelters, so the elite can enjoy their lavish lifestyles without having to share resources with the unwashed masses.

In the sequel, tentatively titled *The Ultimate Truth*, we learn that the entire planet is at war with invaders from off-planet. Earth is protected by one faction in that war, a race of aliens who look just like us and can walk among us. However, this might also be a fabricated war. Perhaps there are no aliens, and perhaps it is all propaganda. A few adepts receive psychic messages from aliens who have important messages for the human race. We feel a tinge of recognition when the aliens talk about genetics; their plan feels uncomfortably similar to Nazi eugenics. They also talk about saving the planet from pollution, from the waste of industry and the garbage of households. They describe humanity as an infestation that is suffocating the planet, and they recommend a significant population reduction. Phil thus demonstrates his prescience: This is decades before the Georgia Guidestones filtered into common knowledge, so you can ponder the prophecy only when looking back at the time you spent with Philip K. Dick.

Phil offers you a shot of single malt Scotch, and soon you are going to need it. He launches into a talk about his *Exegesis*. He has concluded that the universe is a computer and that the computer must be analog, rather than digital. You are familiar with the relatively new digital radios that you can tune to a station through a series of steps moving 10 Herz every time you push a button, or searching for the next station when you push the other button. The old analog radio sets, on the other hand, have knobs that you turn to tune in a station, moving through all possible frequencies in between stations. Phil has deduced the analogical nature of the universal computer from the prevalence of the Fibonacci sequence. From the spiral shape of our Milky Way Galaxy to the spiral growth of a nautilus shell, the Fibonacci sequence pervades all things, both living and nonliving. Thus, the universe is a living thing, a sentient being that creates all the things that we experience. It is the nothing from which everything emerges.

More properly, however, the universe is a living, sentient "no thing". The universe itself is no thing, and it creates every thing. Breaking down the word "nothing" into its component parts, "no" and "thing" helps us to conceive the existence of the vacuum of space.

We say that space is empty, that it is nothing, but it does have existence. The background radiation that astronomers use to prove the event of the Big Bang also proves the existence of space. If space were truly empty, and truly a vacuum, it should have a temperature of absolute zero. However, it actually has a background radiation that has been measured at three degrees above absolute zero.

All the things that we see in our telescopes – stars and planets and galaxies – are actually vibrations. Phil has been reading about string theory. The question is, what is vibrating? No thing is vibrating; the vacuum of empty space is actually vibrating. Pythagoras was correct when he said that the cosmos is made of music and that he could hear the music of the spheres. That music is produced by the vibration of a string, a reed or some other thing. So in a sense, no thing exists and vibrates. Only the illusion of things reaches our senses and leads us to believe that things exist. The music of the spheres exists in a literal sense, and it has mathematical properties.

When scientists try to conceive of a language that all creatures can understand, so we might be able to communicate with aliens from a distant world, they decide that mathematics is a truly universal language. Phil says that the true universal language is music. He imagines an intelligent alien race that has no sense of hearing. They must touch music, feel its vibrations, in order to understand it. Her points out that the lowest note on some church organs is beyond the range of human hearing, at least for most people. We feel the 16-cycle note, rather than hear it. We hear vibration in the sound of rushing water, we see it in the sunlight and we feel it in the rush of the wind. Beneath the surface, however, vibration creates the water, the sun and the air. Without vibration, nothing (no thing) would exist. Conversely, with vibration, no thing (the vacuum of space) cannot exist. And so we have a logical paradox: where there is vibration, no thing (the vacuum of space) cannot exist, but no thing is vibrating. Vibration is necessary for any thing to exist, and every thing is vibrating. How did no thing continue its existence after vibration happened, and what is vibrating, if no thing does not exist? Phil concludes that the 3 degree background radiation arose from the destruction of no thing when vibration began. Thus, the background radiation is vibrating, even if we cannot detect that vibration. Rather than a no thing of empty space, rather than a vacuum, we have a thing that pervades the entire universe. No thing both exists and does not exist at the same time, or at no time, or at any time. Phil is paraphrasing Heisenberg's Uncertainty Principle, and you down the last of the whiskey.

The no thing that we call empty space and the vibration of that no thing must have come into being either simultaneously or at different times. However, since time did not exist before no thing and vibration came into existence, what does simultaneously mean? Simultaneously, or "at the same time", cannot have meaning before time exists. And what does "at different times" mean before time comes into existence? Since time is the relationship among objects in motion, time does not exist without objects. Let us call the no thing, the vacuum of space, a thing, and let us call that thing the medium. The medium, which is a thing, came into existence with the destruction of the no thing caused by vibration. That destruction produced the background radiation, which we erroneously call empty space; it is actually the medium in which all things exist. The vibration of the medium creates the objects and their motion, and thus it creates time. However, we cannot find the origin of the vibration that caused the no thing to cease to exist. The no thing was not an object, and before objects were created, there was no time. In other words, the creation of the universe happened at no time. In addition, the medium is both vibrating and not vibrating at the same time. Phil has been reading up on quantum physics.

Now you are hoping for a second shot of whiskey.

Phil moves on to his theory about the cosmic egg, which he has based on his reading of ancient myth and religion. He is fascinated by the concept of twin deities hatching from a cosmic egg. Already knowledgeable about Gnosticism from his friendship with Bishop Pike in the 1960s, Phil has studied Eastern religions. He finds Manichaeism and Zoroastrianism particularly fascinating.

A week later, he begins to define some terms, which you find useful. "Nothing" or "no thing" can be defined as something or some thing that we cannot observe with our five senses. In other words, it is something, and it does exist, but we can't see it. We know that it exists because we can observe its effects on things that we can see. For example, galaxies do not fly apart, even though gravity is not strong enough to hold them together.

Physicists talk about dark matter and dark energy, but what they are really attempting to explain is the no thing that is the medium in which every thing swims. Most people are not aware of dark energy or dark matter, but Phil has made friends with a physicist, at least through correspondence, since he rarely goes out any more. His crippling phobias severely limit his life.

On your next visit, Phil is talking about religion again. He talks about Sophia, the small female half of the twin godhead. She is filled with love and wisdom, but she has given birth to a monster. Her child thinks that he is God, but he is not. He has created a fallen world, our world. Sophia enters our world and tries to repair it. She tells her secrets to prophets and seers, but the mass of humanity refuses to listen. The world cannot receive her wisdom or her love. The world needs the Savior who is God in human form.

In the beginning, a cosmic egg hatched and twin deities emerged. The male twin was strong, and the female twin was beautiful. Together, they formed the godhead. But something happened that separated them, and each was incomplete without the other. In their desperate efforts to complete themselves, they made worlds and stars and galaxies, but they failed to realize that what they actually needed was each other.

The female twin is called Sophia, which means God's holy wisdom. She inspired the books of the Bible. She wandered among the planets of our solar system, searching for something lost, something forgotten. She failed to remember her twin brother.

The male twin has forgotten his own name. He is the nameless, relentless force of destiny that creates worlds and destroys them. He does not remember his twin sister, but he always feels an empty place inside himself, a space that he cannot fill. He tries to fill it by seeking dark-haired women. His mother told him that his sister Jane had dark hair. In 1973 he wrote a book titled *The Dark-haired Girl*.

You cannot help but see the biographical side of this theology. Phil himself is a twin, and he lost his twin sister. She died as an infant. When he was a child, he used to pretend that he was playing with his sister.

This is so sad that you are beginning to wish that Phil would talk about cosmology again. A sip of French roast coffee helps a little. A shot of single malt scotch helps even more, so you brought him a bottle. Tonight you are eating turkey sandwiches that you bought at Trader Joe's, not steak and kidney pie.

He begins to tell you about his daughters. One is getting married, and the other is entering her senior year in high school. He tells you some things that are too personal to repeat. Phil begins to shed tears about the many years when he couldn't spend time with his daughters. At least he gets to see his son as often as he wants.

In fact, he takes his son to visit Tim and Serena Powers every Thursday evening. On one such evening, Christopher won a quarter in a game. While they were walking home, a veteran with a missing arm approached them asking for change. Without hesitation, Christopher handed the man his quarter. Phil was so proud of his son's generosity that he couldn't wait to tell everybody.

On another evening, Phil begins to tell you about the next novel that he plans to write. This one will be a thriller, or perhaps a hard-boiled detective novel / murder mystery. Something that Robert Ludlum might write, or perhaps something more along the lines of a Mike Hammer story.

The story begins with the death of a millionaire at his house on the beach in Malibu. The dead man has been shot, probably over a drug deal gone bad. He has mob ties, and he has been suspected of smuggling heroin over the border from Mexico. The detective in charge of the investigation begins to suspect that this murder had a more personal motive. He soon finds himself immersed in the world of pornography and snuff films. You find this plot disturbing.

By now, Phil's apartment has become more familiar to you than your own, if that were possible. You know every broken spring in his brown plaid sofa, every snagged thread in its roughly woven fabric. His cat Harvey Wallbanger knows you well enough to be petted, and the calico Mrs. Tubbs often sits on your lap. You look across the living room to the bar that he uses instead of a kitchen table. It serves as a sort of portable wall, since it rests on wheels and is easily moved despite its considerable weight. Some of the steel studs are missing from the black leather front of the bar, giving it the look of a sad but cherished piece of furniture. The glass-topped coffee table is cluttered with all sorts of trivia: magazines, several half-full ashtrays, pens and pencils, paper clips, rubber bands and such. You admire the knickknacks on his bookshelves, which consist of pine boards resting on cinder blocks. He has a ceramic rosy cross that he purchased from the Rosicrucians (AMORC), along with two of their sphinx-shaped incense burners. He has placed in a prominent spot on the top shelf a crudely carved, hand-painted wooden statuette of a saint that he bought from Pier 1 Imports in San Francisco. He tells you that it was made in the Philippines. He wanted his daughter Laura to have it, but she rejected the gift. He thought it would protect her from evil, but she finds it disturbing.

He likes to pose for photos while sitting on his couch directly under his favorite Fat

Freddy poster, which says, "Speed Kills".
Well, at least Freddy tries to say it, but it
comes out, "Keed Spills" and "Pill Skeeds".
He also likes to show you his treasured
possessions.

On the floor beneath the bottom bookshelf,
Phil has placed most of his considerable
collection of record albums. The hundreds
of vinyl LPs include classical music, rock
and roll, Brian Eno's music made on a 30-
foot wire, whale songs, and even a few old
78s on shellacked clay platters, including the
musical "Oklahoma" and songs by Pete
Seeger, as well as a rare recording of Lotte
Lenya. He appreciates all sorts of music, and
his record collection reflects his eclectic
tastes. He plans to buy a reel-to-reel tape

recorder and put all of his music on tape, but he never does it.

The pine shelves are filled with books, some stacked sideways to fit more of them into the crowded space. Phil has at least as many books as record albums. He has several of Franz Kafka's novels, but most of his books are nonfiction. The dust cover of one book that he prizes shows a red mushroom with white spots; it is John Allegro's *The Sacred Mushroom and the Cross*. One of his prize possessions is a leather-bound set of the Encyclopedia Britannica. He also has the books that he used for research in writing his novels; many of those books concern Hitler and the Nazis, which he hoped to use while writing the sequel to his Hugo Ward-

winning novel *The Man in the High Castle*.
He never writes that book. At one end of the
top shelf stands an onyx bookend. It's mate
was lost years ago, so he has only the one.

A metal case with glass doors and three
shelves stands next to the bookshelves,
displaying his most precious and fragile
possessions. He has a trilobite fossil, half a
dozen demitasse cups with saucers, some
rare books of poetry by James Stephens and
a variety of books and trinkets.

His master bedroom boasts a king-size bed
and a clothes closet that runs the full twelve-
foot length of one wall. The second bedroom
is much smaller, with cardboard boxes full
of notes and manuscripts covering most of

the floor. Phil's Olympus manual upright typewriter sits on a typing table. His small swivel chair faces the wall. He says that he likes to eliminate distractions while he's writing, which makes a plain white wall perfect for his purposes.

His bathroom appears to enjoy regular cleaning, but he has left soap scum in and around the sink. He says that he doesn't know how to get it off. You try to help by scouring it with a scratchy pad. You find quite a few clipped bear whiskers embedded in the soap scum. He keeps his beard trimmed short. It is black with gray streaks, which makes him look like Orson Welles.

Phil picks up a pack of Gauloise and offers

you one. He likes those harsh, non-filter cigarettes imported from France, but he also has some Krakatoa Kreteks, Indonesian cigarettes flavored with orange peel, cloves and other spices. Sometimes a clove explodes inside the cigarette and throws burning bits of tobacco all over. His ability to smoke one cigarette and then leave them alone for a week or more tells you that he is a dabbler, not an addict. He does drink a lot of coffee, and he swallows vitamin pills by the handful. However, he has cut back on the heart and blood pressure medications that his doctor prescribed, and that worries you. Phil thinks that the vitamin supplements work better, but you are not convinced.

Phil stands up, reaches into the pocket of his worn blue jeans and pulls out a ring of keys. Handing the keys to you, he asks you to go downstairs to the courtyard and get his mail for him. His agoraphobia is really bad this week, so he can't go outside. Besides, he thinks he has the flu. He tells you that his therapist ordered him to get in his little car and drive over there for his appointment, but he just can't do it. It was all he could do to use the telephone to call up and cancel it. His phobias include a fear of using electronic devices, including the telephone and the television. He refuses to compose his novels and stories on a computer, claiming that the quality of his writing would suffer if it were too easy to type the words. Of course, his phobia contributes to his resistance to even the most simple word processor or even an electric typewriter.

You haven't yet realized that Phil has a serious medical condition that causes him to cancel appointments, claiming that he has the flu. In fact, you figure it out only a decade later, when all three of his children develop the same condition. The doctors never diagnosed Phil's genetic gall bladder problem, and they are at a loss for how to treat his adult children. At first it seems to be celiac, but that turns out to be wrong. The problem definitely lies in a malfunctioning gall bladder, and it affects the pancreas.

You do notice that Phil's hair is thinning and almost completely gray. He looks much older than 58. The hair is receding from his forehead, and he has resorted to a comb-over. He has also lost a lot of weight. His doctor told him to lose 20 pounds, but he has lost 50 and can't seem to gain it back. His shirts, which used to seem about to burst their buttons, now hang loosely. His barrel chest, which he claims is the result of childhood asthma, seems a little sunken.

Most of the time he simply puts on a T-shirt, maybe the Rozz Tox shirt that Nicole and Gary Panter gave him when they interviewed him for *Slash* magazine. Other times he puts on a T-shirt that says that he's an inmate in an insane asylum.

His eyes have lost some of the sparkle that

used to enchant you. He looks pale, and he seems tired. He still gets up to pace around the room once in a while, but most of the time he sits in a recliner chair that he recently bought.

One Thursday evening, he fails to show up at Tim and Serena Powers' apartment. He is found on the floor in his living room, conscious but unable to move. He has suffered a major stroke. After two weeks in intensive care, the life support machine is turned off and his family and friends say goodbye for the last time.

He will tell no more stories.

Printed in Great Britain
by Amazon